Hospice Bed Conversations

poems by

Alan Harris

Finishing Line Press
Georgetown, Kentucky

Hospice Bed Conversations

Where the arts of aging
and listening
meet to sing poetry
and share final words

For Christian Wisner
and
Bruce Bancroft

ACKNOWLEDGMENTS

Hospice House published by *Poetry Breakfast* (2016)
Pearls published by *Metric Conversations (2013)*
Not Today published by *Snapdragon* (2015)
Body Language published by *Pulse* (2016)
Shed published by *Gyroscope Review* (2015)
On the Run published by *Boston Literary Magazine* (2015)
If Stephen King Wrote Poetry published by *The Lake* (2016)
Waiting for something to happen published by *Boston Literary Magazine* (2017)
Black Smocks published by *Boston Literary Magazine* (2017)
In Between Colonoscopies published by *Panoplyzine* (2017)
Life in the Past Lane published by *Panoplyzine* (2016)
PICC-line published by *Temenos* (2016)
Memory Stick published by *Anomolie* (2014)
The Man in the Moon published by *The Tishman Review* (2015)
The Whisper published by *Psaltery & Lyre* (2017)
Waiting Room published by *Nazar Look* (2014)
The Hard Questions published by *Spirits* (2017)
Dead Man's Hat published by *Word Fountain* (2017)

Publisher: Leah Maines
Editor: Christen Kincaid
Cover Art: Calum MacAulay
Author Photo: Amy Ortiz
Cover Design: Elizabeth Maines

Printed in the USA on acid-free paper.
Order online: www.finishinglinepress.com
also available on amazon.com

Author inquiries and mail orders:
Finishing Line Press
P. O. Box 1626
Georgetown, Kentucky 40324

U. S. A.

Table of Contents

Go gentle

I lay in a hospital bed
reading what Dylan Thomas
had cried out to his father
in what would become iconic verse
unwavering instructions
not to go gentle into that good night

and I wonder
what Dylan's father would have wanted
if only he had been asked

as for me
I will neither burn nor rave
at the end of the day
I will not rage
against the dying of light
nor the coming of darkness

for if it's alright with you
into that good night
I will gladly go gentle

Self Help

Don't over-protect me
especially from myself
keep your stainless steel toilet rails
leave my throw rugs alone
I'll put on my own socks
thank you
button my own shirts
tie my own shoes
bathe myself
use the stove and do my own laundry

I'll compromise
for safety's sake
you can take either
my car keys
or my cigarettes
but not both

If out of an
ill-conceived notion
that you know
what's best for me
then at the very least
leave one bullet
in the chamber
of the gun I keep
under the allergy-free pillow
at the head of my
empty marital bed
complete with rubber sheets
side-rails
and an emergency
call button

Pearls

In the nursing home cafeteria
she wears her pearl necklace to breakfast
her fingers caressing each gem
like it was Aladdin's lamp
and as each wish is granted
she travels through time
from pearl to pearl
secretly opening doors to the past

The staff physician blames her age
falsely accusing longevity
for suspending her belief in tomorrow
and precluding any coherent
interest in today
But if science only understood
she doesn't simply
recall and remember
she returns

to call out her lover's name for the first time again
to calm her newborn's fear of the light
her toddler's fear of the dark--
to caress her mother's hand for the last time once more
re-living moments that made a difference,
moments that prove to her heart she was there
moments that ensure her humanity
shining forever
like pearls strung along the thread
of her life-story

Black Smocks

I leave the door of my hospice room
open
the view from my wheelchair
intrigues
green smocks, yellow smocks, white smocks, blue smocks
black
dance back and forth with
purpose

green knows the way to the caf'
and back
yellow knows where the linens
are hidden
white oversees the so-called
vital checks
blue simply volunteers
to listen

but black's a walking reminder
death's on duty
waiting to wheel me away
upon white's order
so that yellow can
change the sheets
while green feeds and blue listens to
the next departee

Not Today

The sand on the beach
recognizes her footsteps
as each grain moves aside
out of respect and appreciation
for her loyalty

Her gait is more cautious
than the year before
as the sea gulls pay attention
in hopes she'll spill the contents
of her picnic basket

The lifeguard tips his sunglasses
as she returns a smile
like strangers do who understand
that there are bonds
in familiarity

All the while waves
flirtatiously caress each foot,
carrying messages from
Virginia Woolf
and Edna Pontellier

But with pockets weighed down
with stories, not stones
she smiles at the invitations
and whispers
...*Not today*

Hospital Bed

The hospice nurse suggested it
my own bed
in the living room
with side rails
so that I won't fall on the floor
controls to raise my head
elevate my feet
a vinyl mattress cover
to protect me
from the previous patron
all the while
my wife sleeps alone
in the other room

I don't like the new sleeping arrangement
I don't like the changes it has made
in my own house
there on the door jamb
left behind by the man
who delivered the bed
is a scratch mark
that will remain long after I'm gone
along with the new sheets
my wife purchased
for the bed in our room
the one without side rails
where I will never sleep again

Dead Man's Hat

I found this hat in the desert
the head it belonged to was nowhere in sight
I shook out the sand
and believe any bugs that had called it home
were thoroughly baked in the sun
along with the previous owner

I call it my dead man's hat
no need for fancy names
I figured one of us was headed nowhere
and the other headed somewhere else
I just wasn't sure
which one was which

Like most relationships
it started out rough
fitting snug at first
until after the chemo
where it waited for me
and we became inseparable

I imagine the previous owners
were ranch hands
if not gunslingers
who proudly wore it
100 years ago or more
though the tag says *Made in Thailand*

Which brings me to an important request
I want you to save the hat
return it to the desert
let it bake in the sun
or if you've a mind to
you're welcome to try it on

Waiting for something to happen

There you are in the hospice bed
wondering if anyone really knows
when it all comes to an end
you thought you did but you don't
they gave you six months
that's what the referring physician
stated in writing
that's what the Medicare reimbursement
is based on

if you live any longer
whether you like it or not
you do so knowing
…number one
you've proven your doctor wrong
again
…and number two
the hospice is taking care of you
for free

Unless there is a miraculous
recovery
which never happens
your time above ground
is more limited than it was before
before the doctor got ahead of himself
before the insurance money dried up
before your friends and relatives stopped calling
because they figured you'd be gone by now

So you wait for something to happen
you up your liquid morphine
you listen to your favorite music
you touch faces in old photos
of those who can still stir memories
despite the medication
and you wonder was it all worth it
and you wonder what's next
and you wonder if you're already gone

Corners and Curves

he proudly explained to me
his life-long philosophy
of corners and curves
it's all about decisions, he'd say
and how we come to them
or avoid them altogether

he was a man of action
rather than allow any decision
to meander along the slow cautious edge of a curve
he cut to the quick, the chase
turned the corner
embraced the commitment

to act now and leave nothing to chance
to get to where he was meant to be
it helped him accept where he ended up
in a hospice bed
where he anxiously awaited the opportunity
to make one more hard right

The Whisper

I heard it again
last night
but no one believes me
so I've stopped talking about it
I even deny it
when they ask
if I am still hearing children at the door

not children
just one voice
young
confident
familiar

whispering
through the keyhole
the same question
night after night

I never offer an answer
I suspect that's because
I'm afraid
but the child is undeterred
persistent
and quite possibly
rhetorical

asking me once more

...is that all there is?

If Stephen King Wrote Poetry

it still goes on
those little things
that annoyed me about you

the casket's closed
but the kitchen cabinets remain open

it's like you're here
going through the junk drawer
leaving the toilet seat up

the dog wags its tail
at your La-Z-Boy

your favorite beer
fills my fridge
your socks lay on the floor

our grandchild
still talks to you

your aftershave
calls my name from
hand towels and pillow cases

the damn lawnmower
refuses to start without you

along with the car,
barbeque grill,
and sump pump

which leads me to
your photo on the wall

as I wonder if those eyes
are asking me to follow
or are simply saying *good-bye*

They're talking about me

There they go again
talking about me
as though I'm already gone
yet remain
the topic of discussions
with everyone but me

They don't want my opinion
that would only hamper
their version of the truth
I'd only get in the way
of treatment plans
or lack there of

Because if I was engaged
in the process
the prognosis
the planning stage would not start with
how soon will we need
this bed?

Hospice House

They've been numerically labeled
all their lives
first husbands, second wives
the last four of their social security number

not anymore--
here each room is the name of a tree
what used to be 227
is now the *Magnolia Suite*

each cold metal door
replaced by natural grains
not a barrier but a metaphor
that swings both ways

reminding us how loved ones
and wood stood tall
through thunder and rain
sunrises and sunsets

asking little but
water and sunshine
provided shelter, food
the very air we breathe

inviting the rest of us--
roots and buds
broken branches
and fallen leaves

to gather together
at the edge of the forest
to hold hands
and face the horizon

for one
final
glorious
sunset

Broken Promise

My father warned me
about unspoken promises
honor and respect
relevancy at the very least
made by naïve children

Now I listen as everyone else
has something to say
but me
and in the clamor
of one-way conversations

they stop to ask
from time to time
if anyone else heard
a faint whisper
an echo in the dark

I do not let on
that the sound
they think they overheard
was something inside me
breaking

Shed

Shakespeare said we shuffle off
or at the very least shed
unmatched socks
worn-out shoes
faded suits
fit for neither weddings
nor the funeral dance

using the Bard's metaphoric
boiler-plated
bullet-pointed boxes
stacked in the cellars
stuffed with stuff
real and surreal
crowding the corners
of our basements
our foundations
clogging our attics
our minds
we check off each item
until the only mortal coil
we have left to shed
is the last breath we take
to say
sayonara, baby

Body Language

after my father had his stroke
we never spoke again
but that didn't stop us
from reading each other's faces

recognizing the punctuated pauses
periods and question marks
etched in eyes, sighs, and sad smiles

It took both hands to hold one of his
that first day in the hospital
as my eyes whispered how much I cared
and his smile replied, *Thank you*

but before I left his side that night
our sighs acknowledged
the painful truth

that despite how well
we finally understood each other
it became regrettably apparent
how little time we had left to talk

Waiting Room

Heaven has a Waiting Room
carpeted and clean
despite old magazines
with God's address cut-out
strewn about
in no particular order
like the souls in line
to have their temperature taken
fearing the scale
because the doctor is in
and he knows the difference
between big bones
water weight
and the heavy burden
of a guilty conscience

Bird's-Eye View

My doctors inspect me with one eye
embracing their version of the truth
their perception limited by
the confines of a single dimension
which they define as
the *standard of care*
with no depth
no texture
simply the flatness found
in pre-Pixar animation
while I am but a 50's cartoon caricature
Wile E. Coyote in a hospital gown
to their feathered protagonistic prognosis
communication void of words
their biased outlook bolstered
by cruel imaginary lines
as they pray for the imaginary train
to pierce the imaginary hole
in the imaginary mountain
standing between us

The Man in the Moon

there's a bench on the moon
where my father sits
reading Byron in the shade

whistling Amazing Grace
smiling like the photo on the wall
whispering my mother's name

while he waits
watching the horizon
for the earth and I to appear

until our eyes
meet
in the moonlight

where we take turns
crying in silence
until we both laugh out loud

Burn

start with the headboard to our bed
then move to the coffin,
my favorite suit,
the blue tie I liked so much,
drawings from the grandkids
the rose you bought
just for this occasion

burn it
burn it all
and let the smoke
enter your lungs
where our memories
will simmer
forever

Amenable

I was informed that my condition
was not amenable to treatment

and as a direct result
furniture was removed from my living room

I suspect the davenport that once belonged to my mother's mother
was not amenable to being put in storage

and if anyone is interested in my opinion
I am not amenable to sleeping alone

on a cold mechanical poor excuse for a bed
facing the television

calling out to visitors and family
to pull up the bedside commode

and join me in watching *The Walking Dead*
as long as we are all amenable

as you tell me how lucky I am
to shit, piss, and eat all in the same room

I was amenable to many things in life
how it ends…not so much

Honoring the Non-Resuscitated

They gathered again in the dining room
of the nursing home
to share whispers and suspicions

Was the old girl dead
when the nurse's aide found her
slumped over her hospital bed-rail?

It's no secret that the nursing home staff
adheres to a strict
Do Not Resuscitate policy

Was she alone?
Could she have lived another day?
Would she have wanted to?

Did she suffer?
When did her family visit last?
What were her dying words?

Such are the whispers
that crisscross dining room tables
awaiting the day they'll find out for themselves

PICC-line

a needle inserted
into a venous cavity
built for the long-haul

transporting fluids
a modern medical miracle
designed to deliver nutrients

or to steal another sample of blood
to measure the ineffectiveness
of the designer drug du jour

it saves poking around by amateur vampires
in hospital gowns
intent to transform me into a pin cushion

instead, they've turned me into
a number on a chart
an occupied bed

another over-medicated dreamer
tubing in the revenue stream
of tomorrow's healthcare merger

floating on a placenta
made of gel foam
and rubber sheets

wading in the darkness
waiting in the light
for the doctor

to cut the PICC-line
the umbilical cord
and send me home

The Hard Questions

The Celebrex bottle is child-proof
much to the chagrin of the children
hiding in shadows
roaming the halls

like echoes
ominous but not threatening
yet nudging her
with silent whispers

to admit that
there's no solace
in sleep
when haunted by questions

like how will she open this bottle
what day is it
will anyone hear
her final words

anyone besides ghosts
regrets
and the bad memories
she shares her bed with

The Magnolia Room

We all die in a room with a dance floor
which smells of magnolias and memories
where inside, music is about to fill the air
by the cover band tuning up to the beat
of the morphine drip stationed at the head of the hospital bed

you can just catch a glimpse of the lead singer
out of the corner of your eye
a young fan of your favorite songs
someone you're sure you've seen before
photobombing your reflection in mirrors long gone

God, ghosts, and demons have set aside their family differences
just long enough to pitch in and cover the bar tab
and as the music starts to play
a line forms on the dance floor
for old and new friends, for family and special guests

to ante up a dollar for the honor and privilege
of one last dance
to two-step across the floor
unencumbered by oxygen tubing
for first polkas and last Tangos

and the only cover charge
is a down payment for the room
to await the day the band returns
with a new lead singer
to play their favorite songs

Memory Stick

I carry a memory stick
on a string
around my neck

My stick archives
1000 images
1,000,000 words

My stick helps me
remember who I am
who you are

My stick helps me
remember the first time
my child walked, talked

the last time
my grandpa laughed,
cried

If I misplace my stick
I may forget
your name, my own

So archive my picture
on your stick, on a string
around your neck

Mention the last time
you saw me laugh,
cry

Carry me with you
until you forget
my name, your own

before your life
is but a frozen archive
on someone else's memory stick

On the Run

Our Indian guide
an experienced tracker
led the posse across the parking lot
hot on the trail
of an aging desperado

until they came upon
a discarded gait belt
an empty bottle of Aricept
and a four-pronged quad-cane
with worn-down rubber tips

but there was no sign
of the outlaw on the run
who had escaped in broad daylight
unnoticed by LPNs
and cctv cameras

they finally sent the posse home
and noted in the police report
that the suspect had avoided capture
with the help of his grandson's
awaiting El Camino

Lost Balance

There was a time
her hair was colored red
she had danced with the Rockettes
she once crossed the Rio Grande
before Roe v Wade
she campaigned for McGovern
she took her children to museums
she taught them to laugh
she survived cancer
a rotten marriage
only to be put on a morphine drip
to ease the pain
caused by a throw rug
left behind by the ex
upon which she had fallen
for the last time

The Gift of Young Visitors

when my grandson stopped by today
it brightened up the hospice floor
to have the voice of a 10 year old
skip through the hallways

as an unwritten rule
they keep children away
making us and death
less visible to the young

but as any grandson of mine will do
he broke the rules
and demanded to tag along
to visit Grandpa

as soon as I saw him
I shouted Bingo!
I knew something good
would happen today

he wasn't sure what *Bingo* meant
as it is rarely heard
in video games
or the schoolyard playground

we came to an understanding
that an appropriate translation
from his grade school lexicon
would be *Boom Shakalaka*

that's the main reason
to allow children to
mingle with the dying
so much for us to learn from each other

Curiosity

On one shore of the river
are the living
casting our fishing lines out
in pure and simple
hope
while on the other shore
our ancestors
cast their lines out of curiosity
for it's not that hope is gone
over there
it's simply irrelevant
and at the end of the day
what really makes us all human
even dead ones
is the unrelenting
biological
spiritual
instinct
of curiosity
wondering what
in heaven's sake
will happen
on that day
when our lines
finally tangle

In Between Colonoscopies

have you ever cleaned your house
by setting it on fire?
that was the first one at 50
the prep was as bad as I'd heard
they sent me home with color photos
of six polyps along with an invitation
to return in two years

up until then
I'd only been high-risk
for eating too much ice cream
for laughing too loud
at The Three Stooges
for crying when Ray Kinsella
asked his dad to play catch

after the fourth colonoscopy the polyps returned
The Three Stooges stopped being funny
I no longer saw myself as Ray
I became his dad
knowing that soon the only opportunity
to embrace second chances would have to come
through cornfields on the way back from the dead

Spirituality

They say the closer to death
the closer to God we become
the hospice pastor believes so
as does the lady with the guitar
the agency sends to sit with me
on Wednesday afternoons

I'm a hard case
says the pastor
that's why, I suppose
I get serenaded with Amazing Grace
on hump days
to let go and let God

But even a hard case can be spiritual
it's just the way I see it, have always seen it
God has never been captured
not the least of which
by old men editing the narratives
of other old men

and now the pastor has stopped coming
because I'm a hard case
a non-believer in meetings with makers
but since I've been wrong before
leave some money in my pockets
enough to buy God a drink

Life in the Past Lane

cancel the MRI
stop the Haldol protocol
I'm not renewing the Namenda
it's neither dementia
nor delirium
casting my mind adrift
it's not depression
driving me back
down old roads
so what if I'm
more curious about the past
than the future
let me return
to my comfort zone
my home sweet home
clean the wax
from your stethoscope
and listen to my soul
you might just overhear
a memory whisper
a professional courtesy
asking you politely
to back away from my chart
and allow my past
to take it from here

I didn't see this coming

this isn't a bad place to be
just not what I expected
the hospice nurses have seen to my every need
it's like a two star hotel with maid service
maybe three stars
but I didn't see this coming
I look around the room
and realize that the only way out is death

I get an idea
if I can't return to the condo with my wife
I'd like to buy a little house
back in my home town
I have the money
I just need believers, friends
and co-conspirators
willing to help me pull it off

but time fades like childhood memories
and while the nurse ups the dosage
of liquid morphine
reality whispers into the confessional
that has become my final four walls
apologizing for the little things
that cannot be
like going back home

Noli timera

I saw an old woman
at cash register
number five
place soup cans
and corn starch
and Raisin Bran
on the moving belt

she turned around
and told her husband
words he'd always remember
...I forgot the broccoli

so off he went
and upon his return
from fresh fruits and vegetables
with broccoli in hand
she laid there on the linoleum
cashed out by death's apprentice
in a grocery store smock

and until the day he died
he heard her voice echo those final words
...I forgot the broccoli
and he was not afraid

$\mathbf{A}$lan Harris is the poet in the hospice ward, unapologetically crafting prosy lyric lines, singing slices of life and death, channeling voices soon to be silenced. Harris has served his community in many ways—as an Easter Seal delegate, American Cancer Society Board member, Easter Seal Volunteer of the Year and most recently the 2016 Sparrow Health Systems Home Hospice Volunteer of the Year. He is a *Tuesday Story Writer*, volunteering to help hospice patients write memoirs, letters, and poetry. Harris received the 2012 Stephen H. Tudor Award in creative writing from Wayne State University as well as the 2014 John Clare Poetry Prize and the 2015 Tompkins Poetry Award.

www.ingramcontent.com/pod-product-compliance
Lightning Source LLC
LaVergne TN
LVHW051608080426
835510LV00020B/3195